Your Body for Life

Health and Disease

From birth to old age

Louise Spilsbury

Heinemann
LIBRARY
Chicago, Illinois

Edited by Andrew Farrow, Adam Miller, and Adrian Vigliano

Designed by Cynthia Della-Rovere

Original illustrations © Capstone Global Library Ltd.

Illustrated by HL Studios Ltd.

Picture research by Mica Brancic

Production by Victoria Fitzgerald

Originated by Capstone Global Library Ltd.

Printed and bound in China by Leo Paper Products Ltd.

16 15 14 13 12

10 9 8 7 6 5 4 3 2 1

Library of Congress Cataloging-in-Publication Data

Spilsbury, Louise.

  Health and disease : from birth to old age / Louise Spilsbury.

    p. cm.—(Your body for life)

  Includes bibliographical references and index.

  ISBN 978-1-4329-7084-0 (hb)—ISBN 978-1-4329-7091-8 (pb)

  1. Health. 2. Diseases. I. Title.

RA776.S697 2013

613—dc23   2012014547

Acknowledgments

The author and publishers are grateful to the following for permission to reproduce copyright material: Alamy pp. 5 (© Corbis Bridge), 14 (© PhotoAlto), 23 (© Image Source), 32 (© Mai Chen), 36 (© Purestock), 45 (Lifestyle Man Medicine Hospital Radiotherapy), 51 (© Jack Sullivan); Corbis pp. 13 (PHIL/© CDC), 41 (cultura/© Hybrid Images), 42 (Visuals Unlimited/© Nucleus Medical Art), 55 (In Pictures/© Mark Makela); Getty Images pp. 24 (Stockbyte), 29 (Taxi/Lisa Peardon), 34 (PhotoAlto/Eric Audras), 49 (McClatchy-Tribune/Chicago Tribune); Science Photo Library pp. 16 (ALIX), 18 (Adam Hart-Davis), 22 (Eye of Science), 25 (Sovereign, ISM), 26 (Eye of Science), 39 (CNRI), 48; Shutterstock pp. 4 (© David P. Lewis), 6 (© Lucian Coman), 8 (© Tsekhmister), 11 (© Fred Goldstein), 12 (© Realinemedia), 28 (© Levent Konuk), 31 (© Suzanne Tucker), 33 (© Sebastian Kaulitzki), 38 (© Paolo Airenti), 47 (© AigarsR), 52 (© Skyhawk).

Cover photograph of lab technician reproduced with permission of Getty Images (Taxi/Noel Hendrickson).

Cover photograph of DNA reproduced with permission of Shutterstock (© sheelamohanachandran2010).

We would like to thank David Wright for his invaluable help in the preparation of this book.

Every effort has been made to contact copyright holders of any material reproduced in this book. Any omissions will be rectified in subsequent printings if notice is given to the publisher.

Disclaimer

All the Internet addresses (URLs) given in this book were valid at the time of going to press. However, due to the dynamic nature of the Internet, some addresses may have changed, or sites may have changed or ceased to exist since publication. While the author and publisher regret any inconvenience this may cause readers, no responsibility for any such changes can be accepted by either the author or the publisher.

Contents

Some words are printed in **bold**, like this. You can find out what they mean by looking in the glossary on page 60.

The World of Health and Disease

Everyone is an individual, and we are different in many ways. Still, our bodies all follow a similar pattern of change throughout our lives. These life stages are birth, childhood, **adolescence**, adulthood, and finally old age. The most rapid changes happen in the first few years after we are born, during childhood, and then during adolescence. Adult bodies change more slowly, but then when we reach old age our bodies again change more rapidly. Our health and our ability to deal with disease change over time, too.

Your body, your life

Health in life is variable—some people get heart disease in their forties, while others remain healthy and active into their nineties.

Life processes

To be healthy during all of these life stages, the body's life processes must all work well. There are seven life processes:

1. *Movement*: When we are healthy, our bones and muscles work well, which means we can move easily.

2. *Reproduction*: Most healthy adults can reproduce, or have babies.

3. *Sensitivity*: Our five senses—sight, smell, touch, taste, and hearing—tell us what is going on in the world around us.

4. *Growth*: We grow and change as we should throughout our different life stages.

5. *Respiration*: Our body converts the food we eat into energy.

6. *Nutrition*: Food provides us with the nutrition we need to perform **respiration**.

7. *Excretion*: We excrete (release or eliminate) waste efficiently.

Various factors—some that we are born with and some that we encounter with age—affect these life processes. Disease is something that stops any or all of the body's life processes from working properly, and so it can affect our health throughout our lives.

Genetic factors

One factor that affects our health, from the cradle to the grave, is **genes**. Genes are inherited from parents: half your genes come from your mother and half come from your father. Genes are made from **DNA**, and they form a sort of genetic code—all the instructions needed to make us who we are. Genes affect our appearance as well as other qualities, such as an inherited talent for music or math. Genes also have an impact on our health.

The genes that people inherit from their parents can cause children to inherit a health condition or disease, or a tendency to develop a particular condition. For example, muscular dystrophy is a genetic condition that gradually causes the muscles to weaken and leads to an increasing level of disability. On the other hand, some of the genes people inherit from their parents can benefit their health—for example, some genes increase resistance to catching diseases.

AMAZING BUT TRUE!

Genes for life

How long you live might partly be determined by your genes. Evidence suggests that a long life runs in families, so if your mother reaches 100, you are more likely to live to celebrate your 100th birthday, too!

Pass it on!
Heredity is the passing of genes from one generation to the next. Genes can affect how long we live and how healthy we are throughout the different stages of life.

Environmental factors

Heredity plays an important role in health and disease, but our environment also has an impact. Environment includes where we live and our lifestyle choices, including things like the foods we eat and the amount of exercise we get. For example, people may have inherited a basically healthy set of genes, but if they are **malnourished**, they may still get sick. On the other hand, people who are at risk of heart disease because it runs in their family may be able to avoid it if they eat a healthy, balanced diet, exercise regularly, and avoid risky behaviors like smoking and drinking too much alcohol.

Malnutrition

Malnutrition is when people do not eat enough **nutrients** to stay healthy. People can be malnourished because they have too little food or because they eat too many low-nutrient foods such as salty snacks, sweets, and fried, fatty foods. That is why people can be both overweight and malnourished. The following facts about malnutrition are shocking but true:

- A lack of food plays a role in at least half of the 10.9 million child deaths each year.
- In 2008, 1.5 billion adults 20 years of age and older were overweight. Of these people, over 200 million men and nearly 300 million women were obese (very overweight).
- Nearly 43 million children under the age of five were overweight in 2010.
- Being overweight or obese is the fifth-leading risk for death in the world.

Your environment counts

Our environment has a major impact on our health. Almost half of the 8.8 million children under five who died in 2008 lived in Africa, where 51 percent of people are living in poverty.

Life expectancy

Life expectancy is the average number of years that people live. In ancient Greece, the average life expectancy was about 28 years; today in Greece, it is about 78 years for men and 83 years for women. One of the reasons people live longer today is because of improvements in nutrition, in the amount and quality of the food we eat, and in health care. New medicines have been developed to treat diseases, and new technologies can diagnose illnesses and cure or relieve symptoms of serious conditions. All of this has dramatically improved our chances of living long, healthy lives.

Different expectations

Life expectancy is not the same around the world. In a **developed country** such as the United States, the average life expectancy is around 80 years. In **developing countries** such as Zambia in Africa, where there is a high rate of **HIV** infection and many people cannot afford to pay for the health care they need, the average life expectancy dropped to 33 years between 1990 and 2000. In 2012, Zambia's average life expectancy was estimated at 52 years.

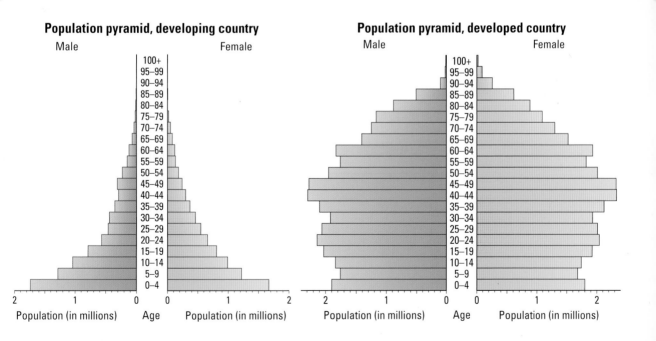

Population pyramids

These are sample population pyramids for a developing country and a developed country. A developing country pyramid is wide at the base and narrow at the top, because there are more young people than elderly people. By contrast, a developed country pyramid is wider in the middle, and stays quite wide until the top. That is because people live longer in a developed country, where health care and nutrition are generally better.

Babies and Toddlers

The first few years of a child's life are an important time in terms of health and disease. As we will see, babies can catch diseases easily, and so caregivers and parents must watch over them very carefully. Most babies are born healthy, but some have health issues that begin while they are in the womb.

The human body is made up of trillions of tiny building blocks called **cells**. A developing baby grows from one cell, which formed when the father's sperm cell fused with the mother's egg cell. This single cell divides and makes copies of itself, and these new cells divide and start to develop in different ways to form the baby's different body parts. As the developing baby, or fetus, grows and important body functions start to work, tiny variations can cause problems. For example, if a fetus does not get the nutrients it needs or is exposed to harmful substances like nicotine in tobacco, the growth rate and function of some of its **organs** may be affected. These changes may increase the risk of certain diseases later in life.

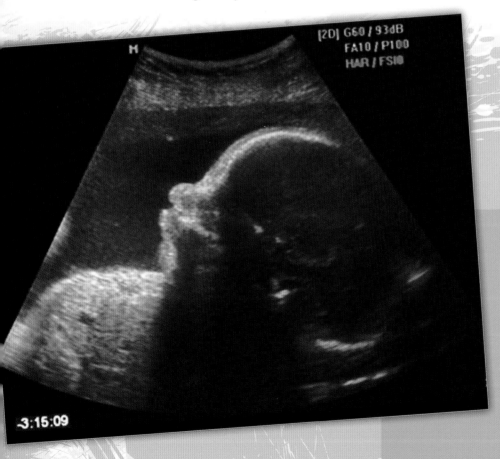

Ultrasound testing

One way that doctors check a baby's health during pregnancy is an ultrasound test. Sound waves are bounced off the baby's bones and **tissues** to construct an image. This image provides useful information, such as whether the fetus is growing at a normal rate, or if there is anything unusual in its development.

Testing newborn health

During the first few weeks after a baby is born, he or she is given a range of health checks and tests. For example, doctors do a physical examination to check things like the baby's eyes, hearing, heart, and hip movements. They do blood tests to check for serious conditions such as sickle cell disease, an inherited blood disorder, and cystic fibrosis, a condition that affects organs such as the lungs (see page 17). Most babies are healthy, but early testing like this means that if there is a problem, children can get early treatment to improve their health and prevent disability or even death later in life.

AMAZING BUT TRUE!

Curing heart problems

A congenital heart defect is when a baby's heart does not develop as it should during pregnancy. It affects 8 out of every 1,000 newborns. Many defects are mild and cause no symptoms, but some can cause major health problems, such as a large hole in the heart (see the diagram). Advances in medicine mean that surgery can correct some severe heart problems that would have killed newborns as recently as 20 years ago.

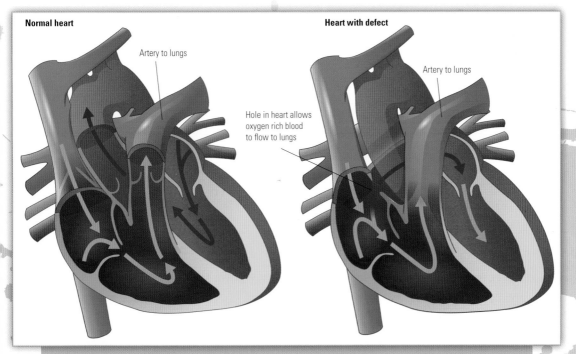

Normal heart

Artery to lungs

Heart with defect

Artery to lungs

Hole in heart allows oxygen rich blood to flow to lungs

A hole in the heart

A hole in the heart usually means that there is a hole in the wall between two of the heart's chambers. Tiny holes cause no problems and heal as the baby grows. Large holes, like the one in this artwork, require surgery. This hole is letting oxygen-rich blood from the left chamber into the right chamber. So, oxygen-rich blood goes back to the lungs, where it has just been, instead of going to the body, where it is needed.

Immunity

It is very important to protect a baby against infection and germs for at least the first 12 months of his or her life, until the baby's own **immune system** improves. The immune system is the body's way of fighting off everyday infections. It is mainly achieved by white blood cells, which are made in soft tissue inside bones (called red bone marrow) and transported around the body in the blood. One type of white blood cell produces **antibodies** that tag **bacteria** or **viruses** when they get inside the blood. Once these invader cells are located, another type of white blood cell finds and destroys them.

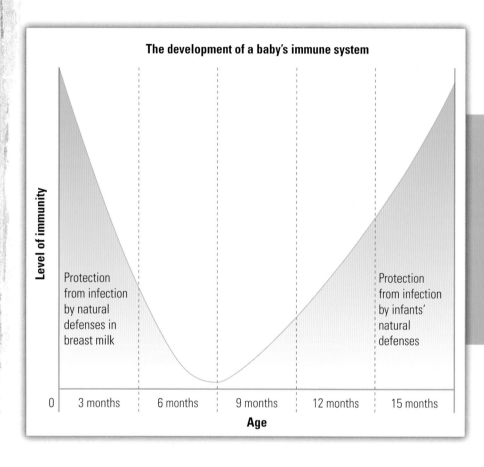

The development of a baby's immune system

Level of immunity

Protection from infection by natural defenses in breast milk

Protection from infection by infants' natural defenses

0 | 3 months | 6 months | 9 months | 12 months | 15 months

Age

A baby's immune system

This graph shows how a baby's immune system develops. It is weakest at around six months of age, when protection passed from the mother decreases and the baby is only just starting to develop his or her own defenses.

Babies are born with protection against some diseases, because some antibodies are passed to them from the mother while they are in the womb. They get additional antibodies when they feed on the mother's first breast milk, also called colostrum. Colostrum is packed with nutrients, antibodies, and white blood cells to protect newborns from some infections. However, they are still susceptible to certain diseases, as they only start to produce their own antibodies after about six months.

Signs of illness

Babies and very young children cannot say that they feel sick, so how do parents and caregivers know if children have an infection—or if they are just throwing a tantrum? After factors such as whether the child is hungry, tired, cold, or has a wet diaper are ruled out, parents check for signs of illness such as rashes, **fever**, and **diarrhea**. Young babies with these symptoms should see a doctor immediately, and young children should also get treatment if the symptoms cannot be treated at home.

Fever and diarrhea

Fever and diarrhea are two common signs of illness:

- Fever is an increase in body temperature that is above normal. It is usually a sign that the body is fighting an infection, such as an ear or throat infection. Parents can make babies more comfortable by cooling them down if they are too hot or warming them up if they get chilled.

- Most cases of diarrhea can be helped by drinking plenty of water. But in developing countries and in disaster zones, diarrhea can kill. This is because a lack of clean water means children become severely dehydrated (they suffer from excessive loss of water in the body). Diarrhea kills around 1.5 million children in developing countries every year.

Taking temperatures

Taking a person's temperature is a way to check core temperature—how hot someone is inside his or her body. Normal core temperature is around 98.6 degrees Fahrenheit (37 degrees Celsius). Someone has a fever if his or her core temperature is over 100.4 degrees Fahrenheit (38 degrees Celsius). When temperature is measured under the arm, it records about half a degree lower than the core temperature.

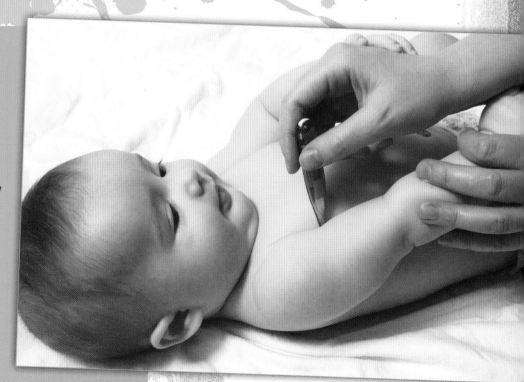

Vaccination

As children learn to walk and to explore the world around them, from petting animals to picking things up in stores, they are exposed to more **pathogens** (germs that cause disease). This helps their immune system to develop further. If people are infected with a pathogen, they feel sick until their immune system develops antibodies that recognize and destroy it. If they are infected again, their body remembers the invaders and can destroy them immediately.

In many cases, doctors use **vaccines** to produce this immunity instead. Most vaccines are a small amount of a killed or weakened pathogen that is injected into the body. The immune system reacts to the vaccine as if it were a real infection, and it develops antibodies that will recognize the pathogen if it enters the body again.

Today, most children are given a series of **vaccinations** to prevent them from developing potentially serious infectious diseases such as diphtheria, polio, tetanus, TB (tuberculosis), measles, and rubella (German measles). It is important that children have their shots at the right age, to protect them as early as possible and minimize the risk of infection. These vaccination programs are standard in developed countries, but elsewhere in the world 1 in 5 children is not fully immunized against the six major killer diseases: diphtheria, whooping cough, tetanus, polio, measles, and TB.

Are vaccines safe?

In recent years, increasing numbers of parents are not taking their children to be vaccinated for some diseases. They fear that vaccines might cause severe reactions or other health problems. But these concerns are based on news stories, not scientific studies. Some vaccines cause mild reactions, such as a slight fever, but overall the risks of vaccinations are small compared with the real risks caused by the diseases they prevent.

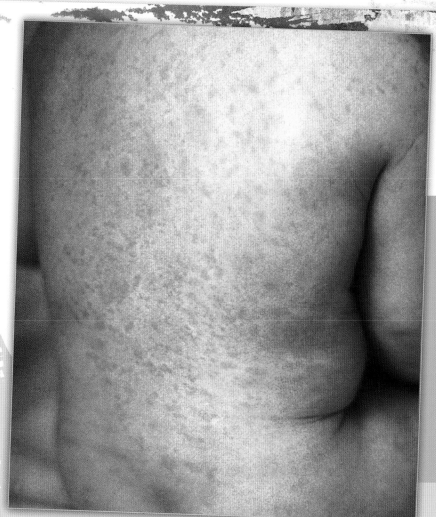

Measles on the rise

Measles is highly **contagious** and, in rare cases, can lead to severe disability among children who survive the disease. Vaccination programs reduced the number of children getting measles in the United States by 99 percent. However, the number of cases is rising again, because some parents think that they should not get their children vaccinated.

Vaccination timetable

The following is a list of common vaccinations and when they are given.

Vaccine	Protects against	When given (months)	
		UK	US
DTaP	Diphtheria, tetanus, and pertussis (whooping cough)	2, 3, 4, 40	2, 4, 6, 15
IPV	Polio	2, 3, 4	2, 4, 6
PCV	Some types of pneumococcal infection	2, 4, 12-13	2, 4, 6, 12
Hib	Haemophilus influenza type b	2, 3, 4,12-13	2, 4, 6, 12
MMR	Measles, mumps, and rubella	12-13, 40	12
MenC	Meningitis C	3-4, 12-13	N/A
RV	Rotavirus	N/A	2, 4, 6

Milestones

Children's development can be tracked by the way they are expected to grow (height and weight) and in the ways they move, play, learn, speak, and behave. Here is a small sample of some of the developmental milestones children are expected to reach in their first five years:

- By two months old: Makes gurgling sounds, turns head toward sounds, follows things with eyes, and holds head up.

- By four months old: Babbles with expression, grasps objects, and may roll from tummy to back.

- By six months old: Strings sounds together, responds to own name, and rolls front to back and back to front.

- By nine months old: Understands "no," makes different sounds like "mama," plays peek-a-boo, sits, pulls to stand, and starts to crawl.

- By one year old: Makes sounds like speech, follows simple instructions, stands, and takes a few steps.

- By eighteen months old: Plays simple pretend games, says several words, walks up steps, and eats with a spoon.

- By two years old: Says sentences with two to four words, names some items in a picture book, kicks and throws a ball, and uses stairs.

- By three years old: Can put two to three sentences together, play with toys with moving parts, and pedal a tricycle.

- By four years old: Sings a song from memory, plays board or card games, and cuts and mashes own food.

- By five years old: Speaks very clearly, counts 10 or more things, swings and climbs, and uses the toilet alone.

Meeting milestones
Being able to hold and scribble with a crayon is one of the developmental milestones most 18-month-old children are expected to reach.

Doctors also use growth charts to track children's height and weight, to see if they are developing as expected. For example, if a child grew at a steady rate until he was four but then began to grow much more slowly, that might suggest he has a health problem. Up until the time babies are 36 months old, doctors measure weight, length, and head circumference. With older children, doctors measure weight and height, and they often calculate body mass index (BMI), which is a number used to determine healthy weight ranges.

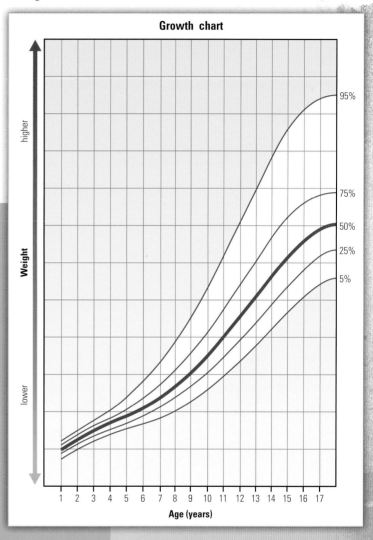

Comparing growth

The curved red lines on this growth chart are measurements that compare a child's growth with others. For example, if a 10-year-old boy's weight is in the 50th percentile (the thick red line), then 50 percent of boys his age weigh less than he does, and 50 percent weigh more.

Most children whose development differs from the average are perfectly healthy—they are simply a bit taller or shorter than normal. If a child's own development line is far off the average, doctors may examine the child to make sure that those differences are not signs of a disease or disability. For example, severe delays in growth might indicate health problems such as diseases of the kidneys, heart, lungs, bones, or other body systems. Differences in the way a child speaks, plays, or behaves might indicate a learning disability.

AMAZING BUT TRUE!

Growth spurt!

On average, a baby triples in birth weight and grows 10 inches (25 centimeters) in length in the first year of life!

Genetic screening

The human genome is the complete set of genes that every person inherits from his or her parents and that is found in almost every cell of the body. The human genome consists of tens of thousands of pairs of genes. Each person inherits one copy of each gene from each parent. The DNA of human genes is about 99.9 percent identical for us all. Changes in a normal DNA sequence can alter the genetic instructions in a person and might increase the chances of inheriting specific diseases.

Genetic testing for **mutations** can be done at any stage in a person's life. If a couple has a family history of genetic problems, they may choose to have a test to determine the risk to their children. Children can have genetic tests to see if they have a genetic condition or to confirm a diagnosis of a genetic condition that has been spotted because of other medical problems. Doctors perform genetic tests by analyzing small samples of blood or body tissues. Many different types of body fluids and tissues can be used in genetic testing. Only a very tiny bit of blood, skin, bone, or other tissue is needed for DNA testing.

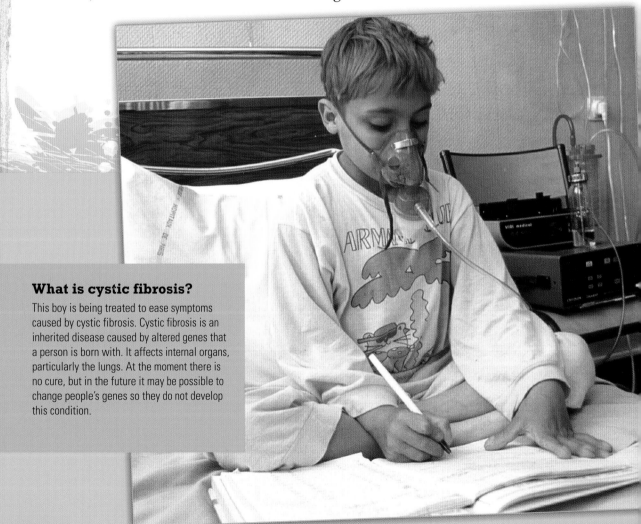

What is cystic fibrosis?

This boy is being treated to ease symptoms caused by cystic fibrosis. Cystic fibrosis is an inherited disease caused by altered genes that a person is born with. It affects internal organs, particularly the lungs. At the moment there is no cure, but in the future it may be possible to change people's genes so they do not develop this condition.

Gene therapy

As research into human genes continues, scientists hope to develop specific types of **gene therapy** to prevent some diseases. The basic idea behind gene therapy is to insert copies of healthy genes into cells with faulty or missing genes, so that the healthy genes will take over. For example, people who suffer from the disease cystic fibrosis get blockages in the lungs because of faulty genes called CFTR genes, which result in cells producing extra-thick and sticky **mucus**. If patients could be given copies of the correct gene, this should solve their breathing problems.

So far, however, there are difficulties inserting normal genes into particular cells without causing problems for the rest of the body, and so current gene therapy research is carefully controlled and does not involve children.

The DNA debate

Some people think that artificially altering our DNA in gene therapy is unnatural, or it conflicts with their religious beliefs. Some fear that if scientists are allowed to develop gene therapy further, it might one day be used to change genes for the wrong reasons—for example, to create smarter or more athletic children—which would be extremely controversial. Supporters argue that we should not ban the technology, because gene therapy could prevent diseases and save more lives.

Helping cystic fibrosis sufferers

This diagram shows how copies of the correct CFTR gene could help cystic fibrosis sufferers. They could be taken in through a virus that goes into the cells like a normal virus. They could also be taken in by a liposome, which is a tiny bubble that people breathe in.

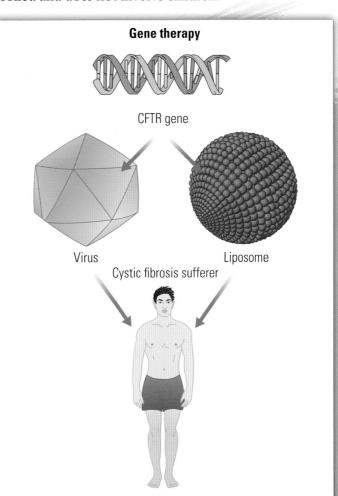

Gene therapy

CFTR gene

Virus

Liposome

Cystic fibrosis sufferer

Childhood

When children start preschool, they are in close contact with many more children—they study, play, and eat together, and that means they tend to get more infections. Two main types of germs—bacteria and viruses—cause most infections. Both usually get into the body in two ways. They can travel on air that contains germs from an infected person who has coughed or sneezed, and other people then breathe in that air. They also get transferred when people touch someone who has an infection or something that the infected person has touched and then put their hand in their mouth.

The power of hand washing

Did you know that 80 percent of common infections are spread by hands? If people wash their hands often and properly (with soap)—especially before cooking, preparing or eating food, and after using the bathroom—this dramatically decreases the frequency of colds, flu, and other infections. It also saves lives. The two biggest killers of children in developing countries are diarrheal disease and respiratory (nose, throat, and lung) infections. Washing hands can cut the risk of diarrhea by almost half, and cuts respiratory infections by a third.

Spreading viral infections

Viruses are too small to be seen by the naked eye, but they can be carried in droplets of **saliva** and mucus that blast out of a person's mouth and nose when sneezing. Children have more trouble fighting off contagious infections than adults, because their immune systems are not as well developed.

Viruses

Viruses cause most coughs, sore throats, and colds, as well as other common childhood illnesses such as chicken pox and measles. Viruses are **microorganisms** that cannot multiply on their own. Once they get inside a body, they enter body cells and use them to make more virus particles. Most viruses cannot be treated with medicines. Patients have to wait until their immune system cures them, which is why there are vaccines for viral infections such as measles. Scientists have developed antiviral medicines for some conditions, such as severe forms of chicken pox, which prevent the virus from multiplying and help patients to get better more quickly.

AMAZING BUT TRUE!

Left out in the cold!

The cold is the most common infectious disease in the United States. Schoolchildren get as many as eight colds per year or more, and having a cold is the top reason children visit the doctor and stay home from school. One reason there are so many colds is that many different viruses can cause colds!

Common childhood illnesses		
The following are common childhood illnesses.		
	Symptoms	**Treatment**
Chicken pox	Red, itchy spots or blisters over the body and a moderate fever	A soothing lotion such as calamine can reduce itching. Severe cases may require antiviral medicine.
Whooping cough	Long fits of coughing followed by wheezy breathing and possibly vomiting	Doctors may prescribe medicine and plenty of fresh air.
Fifth disease	Fever, headache, and very red cheeks; a lace-like rash on the chest, stomach, arms, and legs that can last three weeks	Doctors may prescribe pain and fever medicine and drinking plenty of fluids. The scratching of itchy areas can be prevented by trimming fingernails.
Rash	Usually red, blotchy areas on the skin, sometimes with bumps that may be whitish in color; a child may have a fever	Consult a doctor if a fever develops and if the child starts to behave differently.
Strep throat	Very sore throat, difficulty swallowing, fever, enlarged **glands**, and extreme tiredness	Consult a doctor for tests and medicine.

Bacterial infections

Bacteria are everywhere—on and in our bodies and all around us. Most of these bacteria are harmless or even useful. Some, however, can cause diseases. Bacteria are microorganisms made up of just one cell that can divide and multiply and spread quickly through the body. Doctors identify different bacteria by their different shapes, which they see by viewing them under a microscope (in samples of a patient's saliva or urine, for example). Bacterial infections such as strep throat are usually treated with an **antibiotic** designed to kill the particular bacterium that caused the disease. (Antibiotics have no effect upon viral infections.)

Resistant bacteria

A serious and increasing problem globally is that some bacteria have become resistant to antibiotics and can no longer be killed by them. This is mainly because people have not been using antibiotics properly. For example, people take them too often for things that antibiotics cannot treat, like viral infections, or people do not take the full course of prescribed antibiotics, so only some but not all of the bacteria are wiped out. When antibiotics kill weak bacteria but fail to wipe out any of the strong bacteria in the body, the more resistant bacteria grow and multiply, until antibiotics no longer work on them. Antibiotic-resistant bacteria kill more than 40,000 people in North America a year.

Bacterial or viral?

This chart shows which common illnesses are caused by bacteria and which are caused by viruses.

Bacterial infections	Viral infections
Some ear infections	Most ear infections
Severe sinus infections	Colds
Strep throat	Influenza (flu)
Urinary tract infections	Most coughs
Many wound and skin infections	Most sore throats
	Bronchitis
	Stomach flu (viral gastroenteritis)

Ear infections

Anyone can get an ear infection, but they are most common in children. In fact, in the United States, ear infections are the most common childhood illness after colds. Inside the ear, behind the eardrum (the part that vibrates so a person can hear), there is a small space that is connected to the back of the throat by a tiny drainage tube called the eustachian tube. This space is normally filled with air, but (often during a cold) it can fill with mucus, which may then become infected. Children get more ear infections than adults because their eustachian tubes are narrower than those of adults, which makes it difficult for fluid to drain out of the ear. The immune system clears most ear infections within two to three days, but if it does not clear up and it is caused by a bacterial infection, a doctor may prescribe antibiotics.

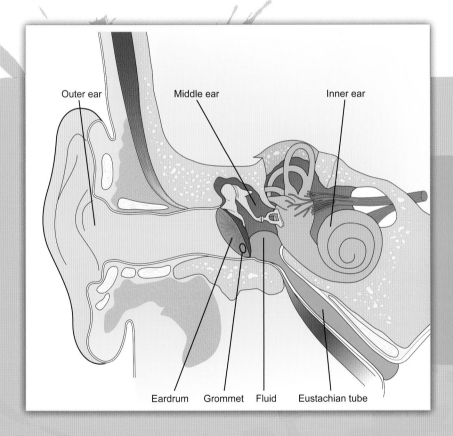

Outer ear   Middle ear   Inner ear

Eardrum   Grommet   Fluid   Eustachian tube

Inserting tubes

In severe cases of persistent middle ear infections, surgeons perform an operation to drain the fluid and insert a grommet or tiny tube across the eardrum to let air into the ear and improve hearing.

Middle ear infections

A middle ear infection is a condition caused when the middle ear fills with a sticky, glue-like fluid. It often develops after a child has had a cough, cold, or ear infection during which extra mucus has been produced. A middle ear infection dulls a child's hearing or even causes partial deafness and a very painful earache. This kind of infection is common among young children, and most cases only last a few weeks. If the infection does not get better by itself, surgeons may insert a tube to drain the fluid.

Allergies

An **allergy** is a reaction by the immune system to a substance that is harmless to most people. Substances that cause reactions are called **allergens**. Common allergens include certain foods (such as eggs, milk, and peanuts), pollen, dust mites, pet dander (flakes of skin from pets), insect stings, and some medicines. The immune system treats the allergen as an invader and releases chemicals, including histamine, into the blood to attack it. This causes allergic reactions, including itchy eyes, an itchy nose, sneezing, a blocked nose and throat, hives (red, itchy bumps), breathing problems, and even shock (faintness or passing out). Some responses are life threatening and can happen when someone comes into contact with just a tiny amount of allergen.

Food allergies

Most children grow out of allergies to milk, eggs, soy, and wheat by the time they start school, but around 8 out of 10 children with peanut allergies continue to be allergic to peanuts for the rest of their lives. Food allergies that develop during childhood and continue into early adulthood are likely to continue throughout a person's life.

Dust mites

Dust mite droppings are one of the most common causes of allergies. Dust mites are 0.01-inch- (0.3-millimeter-) long insects that live in dust all around us, feeding on the millions of dead skin cells that fall off human bodies every day.

Dealing with allergies

One way to deal with an allergy is to avoid the triggers that cause it. For example, someone with an allergy to strawberries stops eating them. But avoiding triggers is not always possible, so some people take medicines to cure the symptoms. In the spring, hay fever sufferers who have an allergic reaction to pollen take medicines called antihistamines to soothe their reactions. Some people are at risk of anaphylactic shock. This is a severe allergic reaction that can make it so hard to breathe that people can die. They have to be extra careful and carry medicine with them at all times, just in case.

Asthma attacks

People of all ages can get asthma, but 50 percent of sufferers are children, mostly boys, under age 10. People with asthma have sensitive airways (breathing tubes), and that means these tubes are often sore and swollen and quick to react to anything that irritates them, from cigarette smoke to dust mite droppings. When the airways swell up, the space for air to get through becomes narrower, and this makes it hard for people to breathe.

Asthma and allergies

Around 80 percent of children with asthma also suffer from allergies. Most children control their asthma by taking medicine, often using an inhaler like the one shown here. These devices allow them to breathe in their asthma medicine, so it goes straight to where it is needed most—the airways inside the lungs.

Broken bones

Another common childhood health problem is broken bones, or **fractures**. Until 14 years old, children are less coordinated and have slower reaction times than adults because they are still growing and developing. They are also more likely to take risks than adults, so as they run around and try out new sports and activities, they often fall and break arm or leg bones.

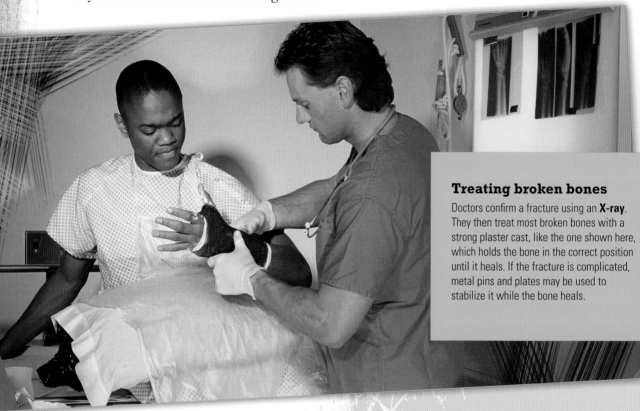

Treating broken bones

Doctors confirm a fracture using an **X-ray**. They then treat most broken bones with a strong plaster cast, like the one shown here, which holds the bone in the correct position until it heals. If the fracture is complicated, metal pins and plates may be used to stabilize it while the bone heals.

Another reason many children get fractures is that their bones are softer than those of an adult. A newborn's skeleton is made of a flexible material called **cartilage**. As the child grows, this cartilage is replaced by hard deposits of calcium phosphate and the protein collagen, which form bone. Bones reach peak strength and density when people reach their full height and stop growing taller, at about 20 years old.

Building and protecting bones

It is important to protect and build strong, healthy bones during childhood, since people start to lose bone density after the age of 30. Here are some tips on maintaining healthy bones:

- Calcium is the chemical that makes bones hard. The body cannot make calcium, so people get it from foods such as dairy products, leafy green vegetables, bony fish, beans, nuts, and seeds.
- Weight-bearing exercises such as skipping, jogging, and walking are particularly good for developing strong bones.
- Wearing helmets and safety gear such as elbow and shin pads reduces the risk of broken bones when playing sports.

Growth plates

People of all ages get broken bones, but only children are at risk of growth plate fractures. Growth plates are areas of cartilage at the end of leg and arm bones that grow in length and then ossify (harden) into bone. Growth plates are important because they help to determine the length and shape of adult bones. Growth plates are the last area of bone to ossify, so they are more vulnerable to fractures. Boys get twice as many growth plate fractures as girls, partly because a girl's skeleton completes the ossification process up to two years earlier than a boy's.

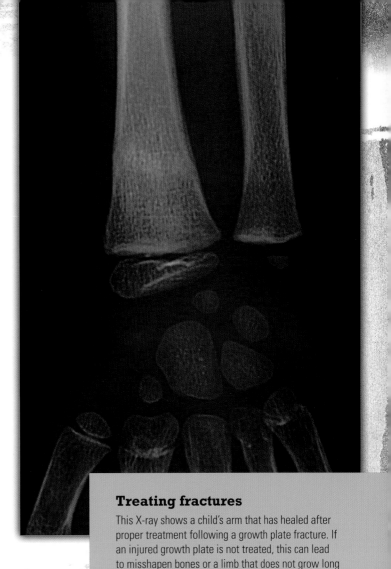

Treating fractures

This X-ray shows a child's arm that has healed after proper treatment following a growth plate fracture. If an injured growth plate is not treated, this can lead to misshapen bones or a limb that does not grow long enough. Most children recover from growth plate injuries with rest and a cast, splint, or brace.

AMAZING BUT TRUE!

Bone blasters

While most adult bones take up to eight weeks to heal, a young child's fracture can heal in just three weeks! While children are growing taller, cells in their body called osteoblasts are working harder than they do in an adult's body. Osteoblasts use calcium from the blood to build bone, so children build new bone to mend fractures more quickly.

Teeth through a lifetime

Teeth start to develop while babies are growing in a mother's womb, but they do not start to emerge through the gums until a child is about six months to a year old. These first teeth are sometimes known as baby teeth or milk teeth, and most children have a full set of 20 by the time they are two and a half.

Braces and retainers

Teeth that are crooked or out of place affect the way a person chews, talks, and looks. They are also harder to clean, so they are more prone to tooth decay. Orthodontists fit braces or retainers that exert a gentle pressure and gradually straighten teeth. These are usually fitted on children, whose teeth are still developing.

At five to six years of age, a second set of teeth, which develop in the jaw, press on the delicate roots of the baby teeth and dissolve them, so that the baby teeth fall out and the adult teeth can come through. Children usually have most of their adult teeth by 13 years old. The wisdom teeth, which grow at the very back of the mouth, do not develop until adulthood. There are 32 adult teeth in all.

People only get one set of permanent, or adult, teeth. Once they are damaged or have to be removed, no new teeth grow in their place. This is why it is very important that people take care of their teeth from an early age. Even a baby's teeth can be affected by tooth decay, so parents and caregivers should start cleaning children's teeth as soon as they appear.

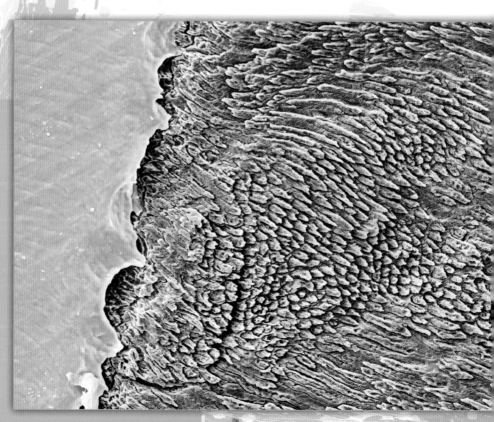

Your teeth, up close

This image shows a highly magnified view of the area on a tooth where the enamel (right) meets the dentine (left). Enamel is the visible part of your teeth and the hardest substance in the human body, but dentine is the material that a tooth is mostly composed of (see the diagram on page 27).

Tooth decay

Tooth decay, also called caries, is the most common disease of the teeth. When teeth are not brushed and flossed properly, a yellowish substance called plaque starts to coat their surface. Bacteria that live on plaque change the particles of sugar and starchy food on teeth into acids that destroy the layer of enamel that covers a tooth. Tooth enamel is the strongest substance in the body, but it cannot be replaced—so once it has worn away, the decay spreads to the dentine and tooth pulp layers under the enamel (see the art). These layers have nerves in them, which is why tooth decay causes toothache. Toothache is painful, but it does warn people to go to a dentist. A dentist can remove decayed parts of the tooth and fill the cavity with a type of white cement to prevent further decay.

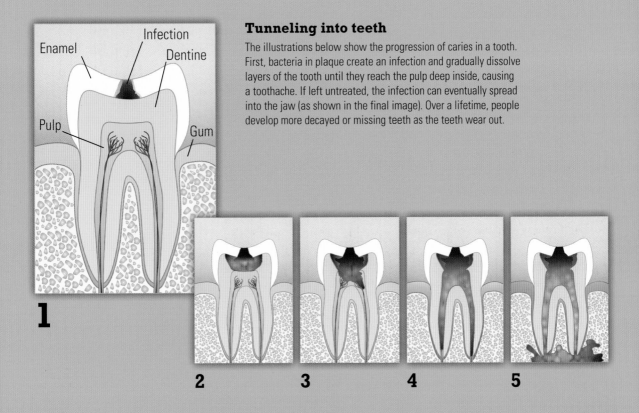

Enamel
Infection
Dentine
Pulp
Gum

1

Tunneling into teeth

The illustrations below show the progression of caries in a tooth. First, bacteria in plaque create an infection and gradually dissolve layers of the tooth until they reach the pulp deep inside, causing a toothache. If left untreated, the infection can eventually spread into the jaw (as shown in the final image). Over a lifetime, people develop more decayed or missing teeth as the teeth wear out.

2   **3**   **4**   **5**

Adolescence

Adolescence is the time between the ages of about 11 to 18 when children gradually become adults. Most adolescents are generally physically fit and healthy, and their immune systems are well-developed, so they get fewer colds and everyday infections than they did as children. However, teenagers can suffer from a range of illnesses and conditions, many of which are linked to the **hormonal** changes that happen in the body during **puberty**.

Teen conditions

There are several illnesses that occur mainly, if not only, during the teenage years, including:

- *Glandular fever (also known as mono)*: This is an infection caused by the Epstein-Barr virus (EBV). It is sometimes called the kissing disease because it can be passed on by saliva. It causes a sore throat, swollen neck glands, and makes teens so exhausted they need to take weeks or months off of school. Most cases affect young adults between 15 and 24 years old.

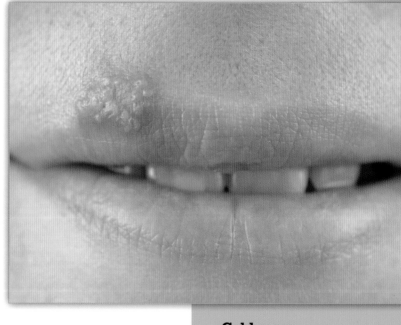

- *Crohn's disease*: This commonly starts between the ages of 15 and 30. An inflammation in the gastrointestinal tract causes diarrhea and abdominal pain. Medicine can prevent symptoms, but there is no cure, so doctors may have to remove sections of the intestines to treat some flare-ups.

- *Cancer*: **Cancer** is uncommon in children. But some types, such as brain cancer and leukemia (a blood cancer), affect more teens than adults, because they occur when cells grow in an uncontrolled way or because a problem with the cells occurs while they are still developing.

Cold sores

Cold sores are caused by the same family of viruses as the Epstein-Barr virus, which causes glandular fever (or mono). Cold sores are very contagious and can be spread by contact such as kissing or sharing a lip balm or lipstick with someone.

Puberty and health

The changes that occur to the body during puberty can have an impact on health. Puberty starts for most people between the ages of 10 and 14. This is when the pituitary gland produces **hormones** that stimulate the production of the sex hormones estrogen and testosterone and the development of the secondary sexual characteristics (features like a woman's breasts and broader hips and a man's facial hair and broader shoulders). For girls, this means the start of the **menstrual cycle**. Lots of girls feel pain or discomfort during periods, which is caused by the womb pushing out menstrual blood.

Anemia

Girls who have heavy menstrual periods can also develop anemia. Anemia is when someone has too few red blood cells. Red blood cells contain hemoglobin, which transports oxygen around the body, so the lack of red blood cells leaves people feeling exhausted. Anemia is worse if people do not get enough iron in their diets, which blood cells need to make hemoglobin. Girls with anemia or low iron levels are also prone to fainting, when the blood supply to the brain is interrupted and people momentarily lose consciousness.

Hannah has period pains, which is why she looks uncomfortable.

Jess has a migraine which is why she's leaving the party.

Jay has a cold sore and will pass it on to Sally while they are kissing.

Will seems to be the life and soul of the party but he's drinking too much and is more likely to be dead from a driving accident than the others at the age of 25.

Future impacts

Adolescence is a pretty healthy time of life for most people, although some have minor health issues and others may start to do things that impact their future health, too.

Mental health issues

The teenage years are full of physical and emotional changes because this is when people develop into adults. Young people start to be interested in sex and become more independent, which can bring them into conflict with parents and other adults. Hormonal changes due to the menstrual cycle also cause mood swings and irritability in teenage girls. Most people get through these tough times, but the stress of these changes causes some teenagers to self-harm, become withdrawn or depressed, or even consider suicide. People in these situations should understand that they can get help from a counselor or sympathetic adult, who will be able to offer support and advice.

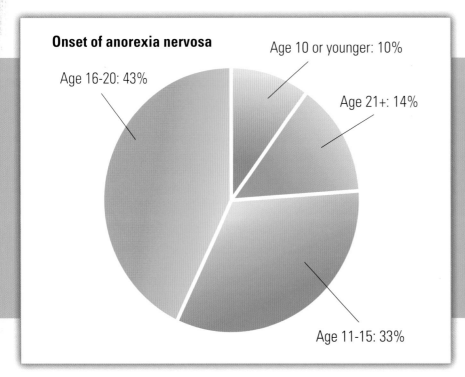

Onset of anorexia nervosa

Age 10 or younger: 10%

Age 16-20: 43%

Age 21+: 14%

Age 11-15: 33%

Adolescence and anorexia
This pie chart shows that the majority of people with anorexia nervosa develop the condition during adolescence.

Eating disorders

Changing body shapes and self-consciousness about appearance can also cause mental health issues such as anorexia nervosa (when people do not eat enough to maintain a healthy body weight) and other eating disorders, which can affect both boys and girls. The main cause of these conditions is low self-esteem and feeling pressure to look thin, which is perhaps why eating disorders are far more common in developed countries than in developing countries. Recovery can take years and can cause long-term problems such as liver damage and bone loss. Eating a healthy diet and maintaining a healthy weight are important for all ages, but especially during puberty. The body needs healthy foods at this time to fuel its growth and development.

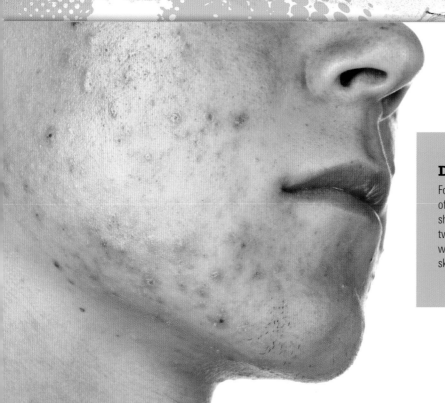

Skin conditions

One of the things that can affect teenagers' appearance and therefore their confidence is acne—pimples that form on the face, neck, chest, and upper back. The skin's sebaceous glands release an oil called sebum to stop hair and skin from drying out. During puberty, these glands make more sebum. In some people, sebum and dead skin cells form a plug in skin pores, and bacteria in this plug produces pimples. Feeling stressed out can also increase sebum production and make acne worse. Cleansing and acne treatments work for most people. To avoid scarring, it is best not to squeeze pimples. Those with severe acne may need to see a dermatologist (skin specialist) for medicine to clear their skin.

Helpful hygiene

Unfortunately, at an age when people are most self-conscious about their bodies, many teenagers also struggle with body odor! That is because one kind of sweat gland, the apocrine gland, only starts to work during puberty. Sweat from these glands does not smell, but when normal skin bacteria decompose the sweat, it starts to smell bad. These body changes mean that teenagers find they need to change their routine, too—showering or bathing more frequently than when they were younger, changing clothes regularly, and using deodorants.

Unhealthy habits

During adolescence, people start to make their own choices, and some of these affect health. If people get into good habits in their teenage years— for example, eating healthy food as part of a balanced diet and getting regular exercise—they might also prevent conditions such as **diabetes**, high blood pressure, heart disease, and some cancers when they are older.

However, these are also the years when people start to explore the world in new and risky ways, sometimes trying things that threaten present and future health. Almost two-thirds of early deaths and one-third of adult diseases are linked to behaviors or conditions that begin in adolescence, such as smoking.

Cigarette side effects
Smoking cigarettes does not just cause bad breath and an empty wallet. It also damages the lungs and causes long-term health problems.

Alcohol

Alcohol is a drug that directly affects the central nervous system, which is the network in the body that relays information between the brain and spinal cord and the rest of the body. So, drinking alcohol affects people's judgment and coordination, reduces self-control, and increases risky behaviors. People who get drunk are more likely to be injured or killed in traffic accidents and fights, from alcohol poisoning, or from choking on their own vomit.

AMAZING BUT TRUE!

Nightmare nicotine

Tobacco smoke contains poisonous chemicals such as nicotine, carbon monoxide, and tar. When smokers inhale (breathe in) this smoke, these chemicals damage healthy lungs and increase the risk of infections such as bronchitis and pneumonia. They also lead to fatal conditions such as cancer (see pages 44 and 45). Today, around 150 million adolescents smoke, and half of them will die prematurely (early) as a result. Tobacco also contains a highly addictive stimulant called nicotine, which makes it very difficult to stop smoking. Around 90 percent of smokers started before the age of 18, and people who start smoking as adolescents have the hardest time breaking the habit.

These problems can affect anyone who drinks too heavily, but adolescents are more susceptible to the effects of alcohol because their brains are still developing. In the United States, for example, a quarter of all male drivers under age 20 who were involved in a fatal car crash had been drinking. However, more teenagers are becoming aware of the dangers. Between 1980 and 2009, the percentage of U.S. high school seniors who said they had drunk alcohol in the past 30 days dropped from 72 percent to 43.5 percent.

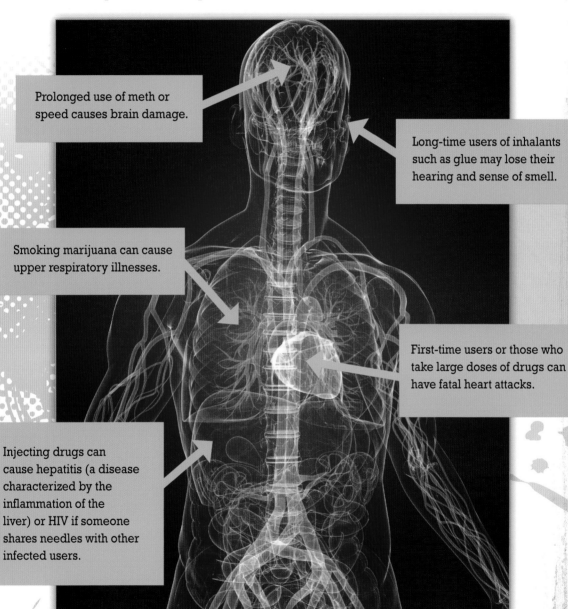

Prolonged use of meth or speed causes brain damage.

Long-time users of inhalants such as glue may lose their hearing and sense of smell.

Smoking marijuana can cause upper respiratory illnesses.

First-time users or those who take large doses of drugs can have fatal heart attacks.

Injecting drugs can cause hepatitis (a disease characterized by the inflammation of the liver) or HIV if someone shares needles with other infected users.

Drug damage

Different drugs affect and damage different parts of the body. Most drugs damage more than one part of the body, and using many kinds of drug carries the increased risk of death or long-term health problems.

Sexually transmitted diseases

Sexually transmitted diseases (STDs) are diseases that are passed from person to person through sexual contact. The best way to avoid STDs is not to have sex at all. The next best way is not to have unprotected sex (sex without a condom). In nearly every case, condoms help to protect against the risk.

STD fears

If someone has had unprotected sex and fears there is a chance they could have caught an STD they should visit a specialist clinic for confidential, friendly advice and treatment, as soon as possible.

Common STDs

The following are some common STDs and the health problems they cause.

Chlamydia

This is a bacterial infection that causes a whitish discharge and pain when urinating. Women may also get abdominal pain, heavier periods or bleeding between periods, and even **infertility**. Chlamydia can be treated with antibiotics.

HIV/AIDS

This is a virus that weakens the body's ability to fight infections and cancer. **AIDS** is the final stage of HIV, when the body can no longer fight life-threatening infections. No cure is available, but treatments enable many people with the virus to live a long and healthy life.

Syphilis

This is a bacterial infection that causes sores on the genitals or mouth, a skin rash, and a sore throat. It can be treated with antibiotics, but it can lead to serious conditions such as stroke, paralysis, blindness, or death.

Gonorrhea

This is a bacterial infection that can cause a discharge from the vagina or penis and pain when urinating. It can be treated with antibiotics, but if left untreated, it can lead to serious long-term health problems and infertility.

Most STDs can be treated, but they need to be caught early. If left untreated, they can be painful, and in some cases they can permanently damage health and **fertility**. In the United States and many other developed countries, young people between the ages of 16 and 24 years old are most at risk of being diagnosed with an STD.

STDs and pregnancy

STDs can be uncomfortable and threaten the health of anyone, but they can be even more serious for a pregnant woman and her baby. A pregnant woman with an STD can suffer the same problems as anyone else with an STD, and she can infect her baby before, during, or after the baby's birth. For example, syphilis can infect the baby while it is in the womb, and gonorrhea and chlamydia can be transmitted from the mother to the baby as it is born. (See the chart for information about these STDs.) HIV can infect the baby at both these stages and, unlike most other STDs, can also infect the baby through breastfeeding.

Most of these conditions can be prevented if the mother is tested for STDs and the baby gets the correct treatment early in the pregnancy. The problem is that many STDs are hard to detect and so may go unnoticed until it is too late. Also, in developing countries, many women do not have access to tests and treatment. If not treated early, babies can be born sick, underweight, and even dead.

AMAZING BUT TRUE!

HIV treatment

In 2009, only about half of the pregnant women living with HIV in developing countries received medicine to prevent them from transmitting the virus to their babies. In that year, about 1,000 babies were infected with HIV every day during pregnancy, birth, or breastfeeding.

Adulthood

After puberty and adolescence, people in their twenties are physically mature and their bodies are probably at their peak stage of health. This is also when people are most fertile, or able to have babies, so many couples have babies during their twenties. Most people stay fairly healthy in their thirties, but after age 40, muscle tissue and bone strength gradually decline and other health issues can develop.

Pregnancy and birth

Fertility is a sign of good health, and most women go through pregnancy and childbirth fairly easily. Some even say they feel healthier than ever before. Some women experience minor problems, such as vomiting, leg swelling, constipation (difficulty with bowel movements), backache, and fatigue (feeling tired).

Health benefits of pregnancy

Most women are healthy while pregnant, and many even find that it has health benefits, too. For example, pregnancy seems to reduce a woman's chances of contracting breast and ovarian cancers later in life, and some research suggests that breastfeeding for more than three months can also lower the risk of certain cancers, although scientists are not sure why.

However, some women have problems that are more serious. During pregnancy, ligaments (tissues connecting bone to other bones) in the body loosen to prepare for birth, but this increases the risk of **joint** injuries such as sprains. Pre-eclampsia is the most common dangerous condition. It causes an abnormal increase in blood pressure and can kill mothers and babies. Medical advances mean that giving birth is safe for most women in developed countries. But in developing countries, over 350,000 women die every year from complications during pregnancy or childbirth.

Diabetes

As adults get older, many become less active and therefore gain weight. This leads to an increased risk of type 2 diabetes, a condition in which there is too much glucose (a type of sugar) in the blood. The body's digestive system breaks food down into glucose, which enters the blood. When glucose enters the blood, the pancreas gland behind the stomach releases the hormone insulin. This helps move glucose out of the blood and into cells, where it is broken down to produce energy. With type 2 diabetes, the body does not make enough insulin to function properly, or the body's cells do not react to insulin. This makes people feel tired all the time. Most people control their symptoms by eating a healthy diet and monitoring their intake of carbohydrates (starchy foods like bread and pasta) and blood glucose level.

Diabetes dangers

Diabetes is a serious condition because over the years, high blood glucose can damage the nerves and blood vessels. In some cases, this can lead to problems such as gum infections, nerve problems, heart disease, kidney disease, and blindness.

The prevalence of types 1 and 2 diabetes

Type 1 diabetes is usually diagnosed in children and young people. In type 1 diabetes, cells of the pancreas no longer make insulin, because the body's immune system has attacked and destroyed them. Treatment includes taking shots of insulin linked to food intake.

Type 2 diabetes is the most common form of the disease. Type 2 diabetes has a variety of causes, but it is often linked to an unhealthy lifestyle. Type 2 diabetes causes the body to respond incorrectly to insulin, which results in an insufficient amount of insulin entering the bloodstream (see diagram). Children can develop type 2 diabetes, but it is more commonly developed slowly during adulthood. Some doctors recommend that everyone over 45 years old be tested for it.

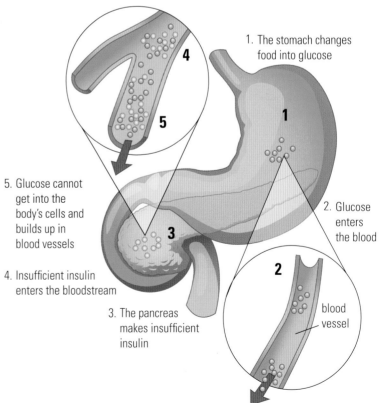

How type 2 diabetes works

1. The stomach changes food into glucose

2. Glucose enters the blood

3. The pancreas makes insufficient insulin

4. Insufficient insulin enters the bloodstream

5. Glucose cannot get into the body's cells and builds up in blood vessels

blood vessel

Heart disease

Another condition that usually begins in middle age is heart disease. The heart is a pump that forces blood through the **arteries** and other blood vessels that carry blood around the body. Blood takes digested food and oxygen to the other parts of the body, so that respiration can take place. This is the chemical reaction that happens in all living cells, releasing energy from food to keep cells—and therefore the entire body—working.

Blood pressure is the pushing force of blood in the arteries. High blood pressure, also called hypertension, means that a person's blood pressure is constantly higher than it should be. This is more common in older people, because arteries tend to narrow and become less elastic (flexible) over time; this means the heart has to work harder to pump blood through. When blood pressure is too high, this puts a strain on the coronary arteries (arteries into the heart) and on the heart itself. This can cause an artery to split or the heart to fail—and, in the case of a heart attack, to stop working altogether. Heart disease kills about 17 million people worldwide every year.

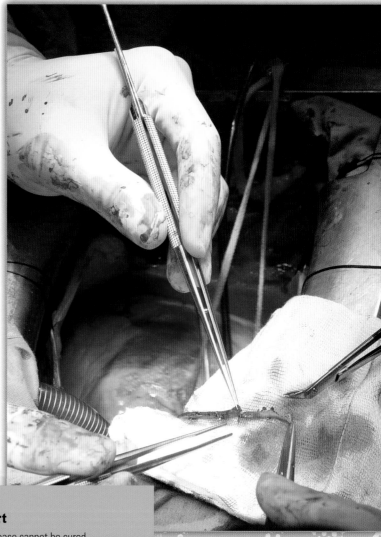

Have a heart

Although heart disease cannot be cured, lifestyle changes, medicine, and surgery to bypass the diseased arteries can improve the functioning of the heart. A small number of people with severe heart failure may have a heart transplant. This is when surgeons remove a diseased heart and replace it with a donor's healthy heart.

Controlling cholesterol

Although heart problems usually begin in middle age or later, they are often caused by behaviors begun during adolescence. Smoking, being overweight because of lack of exercise, and eating a poor diet cause a buildup of fatty substances on the walls of the arteries. These deposits are made up of **cholesterol** and other waste substances, and they contribute to the narrowing of the arteries and thus further restrict the flow of blood.

To help reduce cholesterol levels, people should limit the amount of saturated fats they eat. This kind of fat is found in butter, pies, cakes, fatty meats, sausage and bacon, cheese, and cream. Once inside the body, the liver turns this fat into cholesterol.

AMAZING BUT TRUE!

Reducing the risk

Research suggests that simply by replacing fried and salty foods with healthier alternatives and eating plenty of fruits and vegetables, people can reduce their blood pressure, lower the cholesterol levels in their blood, and reduce their risk of a heart attack by more than one-third!

Other steps that people should take to control or prevent heart problems include:

- avoiding or stopping smoking
- losing weight
- exercising regularly
- avoiding or (as an adult) limiting alcohol intake
- eating a healthy, balanced diet
- limiting salt intake and avoiding foods such as packaged meals that are high in salt
- when needed, taking statins (drugs that lower cholesterol levels)

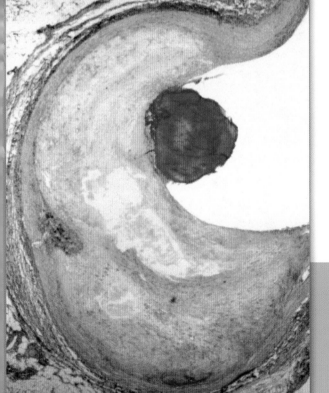

Inside arteries

Cholesterol in the blood hardens and clogs arteries. This photo shows a close-up of an artery that is badly blocked by cholesterol (colored brown here). The red spot is a blood clot that has started to form and further block blood flow in the artery. If the artery becomes completely clogged, the patient could have a heart attack.

Immunity problems

There are over 80 **autoimmune disorders**, and the majority of them affect middle-aged people. With an autoimmune disorder, a fault in someone's immune system makes the body produce autoantibodies that attack normal cells by mistake. This is different from an allergy, in which the immune system reacts to an outside substance that it normally would ignore. What causes them is unknown. They cannot be cured, but medicines can control or reduce the immune system's response. Treatment varies among different types.

Autoimmune disorders
This chart shows some autoimmune disorders and how they affect people.

Disease	Symptoms
Celiac disease is triggered by gluten, a substance found in wheat, rye, and barley, which causes the immune system to damage the small intestine.	Abdominal bloating and pain, diarrhea or constipation, weight loss or gain, fatigue, missed menstrual periods, itchy skin rash, infertility, or miscarriages.
With inflammatory bowel diseases (IBDs), the immune system inflames the digestive tract.	Abdominal pain and diarrhea; some people also have rectal bleeding, fever, weight loss, fatigue, mouth ulcers, and painful bowel movements.
With multiple sclerosis (MS), the immune system attacks the protective coating around the nerves, affecting the brain and spinal cord.	Weakness and trouble with coordination, balance, speaking and walking, paralysis, tremors, numbness, and tingling.
In rheumatoid **arthritis** (see page 51), immune reactions cause the inflammation of joints and surrounding tissues. It can also affect other organs.	Painful, stiff, swollen, and deformed joints and reduced movement and function; it may also cause fatigue, fever, weight loss, lung disease, and anemia.

Menopause

Menopause is the time in a woman's life between about 45 to 55 when her ovaries stop making eggs and produce less and less estrogen and progesterone hormones. Periods occur less often and eventually stop altogether. Changes in the two hormones during menopause cause physical and emotional symptoms, such as hot flashes, night sweats, and irritability. These symptoms are usually annoying rather than disabling or dangerous, and most women get through menopause without needing to see a doctor.

However, hormonal changes can also cause more significant health problems such as osteoporosis, a disease that makes bones fragile and prone to break more easily. Some women are encouraged to take calcium supplements to counteract this problem as well as vitamin D supplements, which help the body absorb the calcium that bones need.

Exercise during menopause

Regular exercise is important at all stages of life. For women going through menopause, exercise helps to strengthen bones, increases feelings of well-being, and can improve sleep patterns, which are often disturbed at this time, too.

Hormone replacement therapy

Hormone replacement therapy (HRT) medicine is used to supplement low levels of estrogen and progesterone hormones during menopause. This lessens the effects of menopause symptoms and can protect bones from osteoporosis, because estrogen aids healthy bone growth. However, HRT is the subject of some controversy because there are fears that certain types could slightly increase the risk of breast cancer, heart disease, and stroke in some women. There has been conflicting research on this subject, but many doctors believe that, if used, it should be at the lowest dose that controls symptoms and for the shortest time possible.

Osteoporosis

Bone is a living tissue that constantly repairs itself. Two kinds of cells are always at work in our bones: osteoblasts build new bone (see page 25), while osteoclasts break down old, worn-out bone. Up until people are in their mid-twenties, the osteoblasts work harder, building bone length and strength. From around age 30 onward, osteoclasts are more active, and bones gradually lose density. If too much bone is broken down, osteoporosis occurs, making bones so fragile that they break easily. In the worst cases, a cough or a sneeze may be enough to fracture a rib or collapse a vertebra (bone of the spine).

AMAZING BUT TRUE!

Essential exercise

While it can affect people of any age, 1 in 2 women and 1 in 5 men over the age of 50 will break a bone mainly because of osteoporosis. But, amazingly, less than half (44 percent) of young people know that a simple thing like exercise can help to reduce their risk of developing it!

Anyone can get osteoporosis, and it can run in families. But, overall, more women get osteoporosis than men. This is because women have smaller bones to start with, and the drop in estrogen during menopause causes bones to thin more quickly. It is estimated that the average woman loses up to 10 percent of her bone mass in the first five years of menopause, which is why doctors usually check women for osteoporosis during this time of their life and sometimes prescribe medicines to treat it.

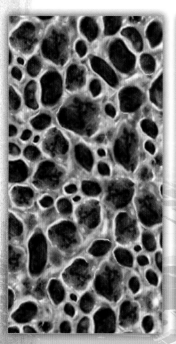

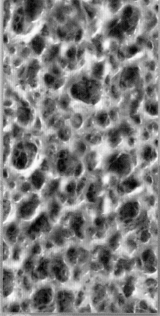

Hole-y bones

The word osteoporosis means "porous bones." Healthy bones (like the one on the right) are very dense, and the spaces within bones are small. In bones affected by osteoporosis (like the one on the left), the spaces (or pores) are larger, making the bones much weaker.

Experiences of osteoporosis

"Being told that you have the bones of a 70 year old at the age of 45 is something I never expected … I remember my grandmother having osteoporosis when I was a child, because she actually had a small hump on her back. I never realized that hump was from the discs in her back breaking and disintegrating, but now I completely understand why I have actually shrunk an inch over the past few years."

—Carol, 45

"I was enjoying a family vacation in the Dominican Republic when three of my vertebrae shattered. Initially doctors suspected bone cancer, but after almost a year I was finally diagnosed with osteoporosis. They told me I had the bones of an 80 year old. I was only 43."

—Robert, 49

"Osteoporosis runs in my family so I know that I'm at an increased risk of developing it when I'm older. I'm in my twenties, which is the right age to bank my bones. I have a healthy diet with lots of calcium, I make sure that I keep my vitamin D topped up, and last year I ran a marathon, because running is a great weight-bearing exercise. I'm thankful that I can do all of these things while I'm still at an age where it makes a difference."

—Carina, 28

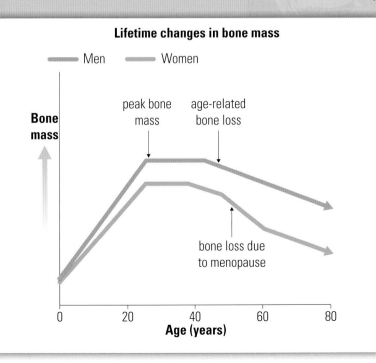

Lifetime changes in bone mass

Men   Women

Bone mass

peak bone mass

age-related bone loss

bone loss due to menopause

Age (years)

Bone density

This graph shows how our bones build and lose density over a lifetime.

Old Age

Many older people lead active, healthy lives enriched by years of experience and learning. Many older adults stay healthy into their seventies and feel well and happy because they have learned to avoid or deal with things that make them feel stressed. When people retire from work, they also have more time to enjoy exercise and hobbies. Many retired people even take up new sports that they continue into their nineties. However, old age is also the time when the way people treated their bodies up to this point can have a major impact on health, and there is a higher risk of age-related diseases.

Cancer

Cancer is the name for a group of diseases caused by abnormal cells. The problem starts with one cell that grows abnormally because of damage to its DNA. This damage can be inherited, it can happen during cell division, or it can happen because of environmental factors such as smoking or catching a viral disease. When this cell divides, it passes on the abnormality to new cells.

AMAZING BUT TRUE!

Cancer cases

Between 2000 and 2010, 12 million new cancer cases were diagnosed worldwide each year, and the disease affected 1 in every 3 people in developed countries. In 2008, cancer was estimated to account for around 14 percent of all deaths worldwide.

Cancer risks

These behaviors increase the risk of cancer:

- Smoking: Cigarette smoke is full of chemicals that attack and damage DNA, which leads to mutations in lung cell genes. In time, this leads to lung cancer.
- Alcohol: Alcohol is the second-biggest risk factor for cancers of the mouth and throat, and too much alcohol often leads to liver cancer.
- Sun: While the body needs sunlight to produce vitamin D, prolonged exposure to ultraviolet (UV) radiation in sunlight can damage DNA in skin cells and cause skin cancer. Tanning beds increase the risk, too.
- Poor diet: A poor diet that includes too many calories, too much red meat, too many processed foods, and a lack of fiber increases the risk of bowel or colon cancer.
- Viruses: Contracting certain viruses through sexual activity or by sharing needles to inject drugs increases the risks of certain cancers.

Eventually, the abnormal cells form a mass of tissue called a tumor. As tumors grow, they invade and destroy nearby healthy tissues and damage and destroy organs. Cancer treatments include surgery to remove the tumor, chemotherapy medicine to kill cancer cells, and radiation therapy, which is the controlled use of high-energy X-rays.

People of all ages can get cancer, but the chances of getting most types increase with age. This may be because cancer is caused by a buildup of mutations that eventually produce an abnormal cell capable of uncontrolled growth. Older people are also more vulnerable because they have been exposed to carcinogens (cancer-causing agents) such as tobacco, alcohol, and bad diet for longer.

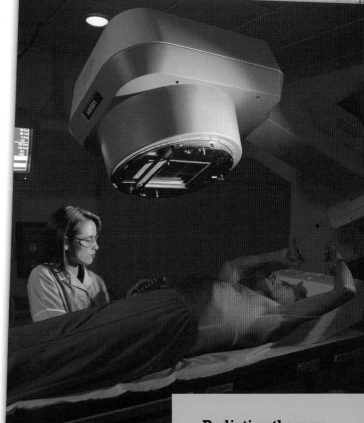

Radiation therapy

Radiation therapy can be used to shrink or destroy a tumor. However, it can also have unpleasant side effects, such as sickness, hair loss, and tiredness.

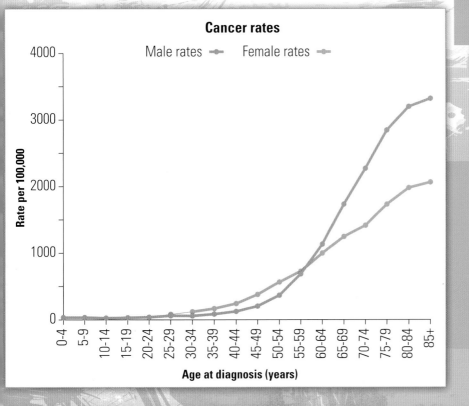

Cancer rates

Male rates — Female rates —

Rate per 100,000

4000

3000

2000

1000

0

0-4 5-9 10-14 15-19 20-24 25-29 30-34 35-39 40-44 45-49 50-54 55-59 60-64 65-69 70-74 75-79 80-84 85+

Age at diagnosis (years)

Increasing cancer risk

This chart shows the average rate of new cases of cancer per year for a typical year, as well as the age at which most cases happen.

Sight problems

As people get older, their eyesight gets worse, and almost everyone over the age of 65 ends up wearing glasses. The main cause for this is changes in the lens of the eye. In children, the lens is flexible and changes shape easily to focus on distant and near images. As people get older, the lens loses this elasticity and its ability to focus over a range of distances. As the lens hardens with age, it tends to fix on distant objects, not near ones. That is why many older people need to wear reading glasses.

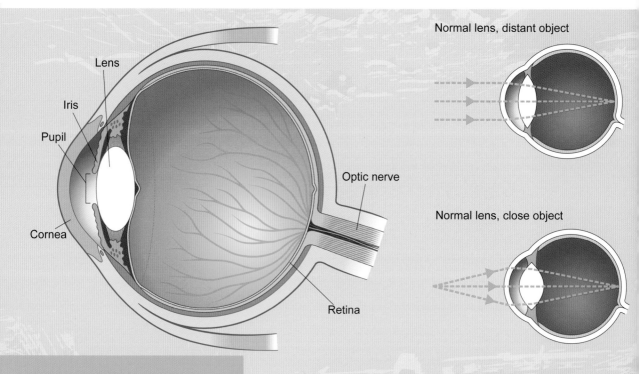

Lens

Iris

Pupil

Cornea

Optic nerve

Retina

Normal lens, distant object

Normal lens, close object

How your eyes work

The large diagram shows some of the main structures inside an eye. The smaller diagrams show how a healthy eye's lens changes shape to focus on objects at different distances.

The lens is made up of mostly water and protein. At birth, it is completely clear, but as people get older, the protein may clump together to form something called a cataract, which clouds a small area of the lens. If the lens is cloudy from a cataract, the image people see is blurred. Cataracts occur in 50 percent of people between the ages of 65 and 74, and in 70 percent of people over 75.

How cataracts work

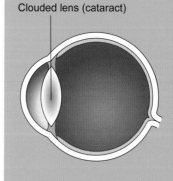

Clouded lens (cataract)

Muscles in the iris (the colored part of the eye) control how much light enters the eye through the tiny gap in the iris called the pupil. The lens adjusts this light, so the image that it focuses on the retina at the back of the eye is clear. The retina changes light into nerve signals that are sent to the brain via the optic nerve. Cataracts affect vision because they cloud the lens.

Turn it down!

Exposure to excessive noise is a major—but avoidable—cause of permanent hearing loss worldwide. The man in the photo is risking his hearing by not wearing proper ear protection. To protect hearing, people of all ages should be careful to avoid noises that are too loud, too close, or last too long.

Hearing loss

Ears are amazing! We hear because microscopic and delicate hair cells in the cochlea convert sound energy into signals that travel to the brain. After the age of about 60, there is a gradual loss of cochlear hair cells, and this eventually leads to hearing loss or even deafness. The other main cause of hearing loss is exposure to loud sounds such as sound systems and headphones, heavy traffic, power tools, and lawnmowers. Over time, repeated exposure to loud noises weakens and damages hair cells.

Hearing loss can be reduced by the use of hearing aids, but poor people in many countries across the world cannot afford to buy them or even to pay doctors to tell them what type they need. In developing countries, fewer than 1 in 40 people who need a hearing aid has one.

AMAZING BUT TRUE!

Deafness on the rise

Although hearing loss is usually linked to old age—at age 65, 1 in 3 people has hearing loss—it is affecting people at younger and younger ages. In the United States, for example, the number of children three years old and older with some form of hearing loss has more than doubled since 1971. Noise-induced deafness is increasing worldwide because there are more and more machines in use, from computers to MP3 players, making more and more noise.

Respiratory problems

As people get older, their arteries and other blood vessels continue to narrow and lose their elasticity (see pages 38 and 39). That means blood is not pumped around the body as efficiently as it was, and older people may feel breathless because they do not get the oxygen they need. As people get older, chest muscles also lose strength and lungs weaken, and conditions such as emphysema may develop.

Emphysema is a common lung disease that makes sufferers breathless and more prone to chest infections. Some people even die because breathing becomes impossible. Emphysema is caused by damage to the alveoli. Alveoli are tiny sacs at the end of our bronchi, the breathing tubes that carry oxygen (air) to our lungs. Oxygen goes down these tubes into the alveoli, and it then passes into capillaries (tiny blood vessels) that surround the alveoli. Blood then carries oxygen around the body so that respiration can take place. Damaged alveoli cannot work properly.

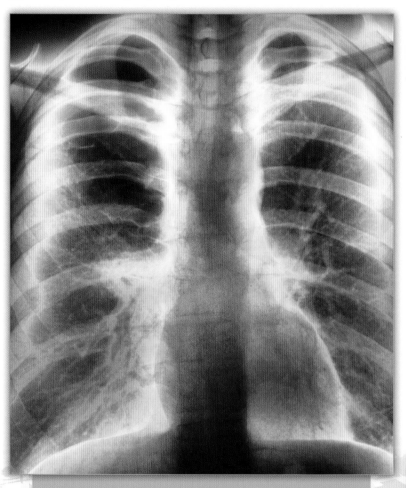

Emphysema

Emphysema is most often caused by years of heavy smoking—although it can be hereditary, which means younger people can get it, too. This X-ray shows an emphysema patient. Emphysema causes trapped bubbles of air in areas of the lungs (shown in green, at top).

Bronchitis

Bronchitis is an inflammation of the bronchial tubes that causes over-production of mucus, wheezing, and a cough. People often get it after a cold or flu or because dust or other irritants get into their breathing tubes. It usually clears up by itself. Anyone can get bronchitis, but old people and young children are most vulnerable to infection. Smokers may get chronic bronchitis, which will not clear up and often occurs with emphysema.

Parkinson's disease

Parkinson's disease makes people less able to direct or control their movements, causing problems with activities such as talking, walking, swallowing, and writing. The disease kills the nerve cells in the brain that produce dopamine. Dopamine is a chemical that allows messages to be sent to parts of the brain that coordinate movement. As levels of dopamine fall, the condition gets worse. As Parkinson's progresses, one-third of those affected by the disease develop dementia. Dementia is a loss of brain function, and sufferers need a lot of care and support.

The average age people are diagnosed with Parkinson's disease is 60, and it rarely affects people under 40—although people as young as 18 can get it. No one is entirely sure what causes Parkinson's disease. However, some scientists think that it may be triggered by exposure to pollutants, in this case possibly to pesticides (chemicals used to kills pests) and herbicides (chemicals used to kill plants), as well as genetic factors. There is currently no cure for Parkinson's, but those who develop it can take medicines to increase dopamine levels in the brain.

Stem cells and dementia

Stem cells are a type of human cell that can develop into different types of cell. In 2011, scientists managed to use some stem cells to grow brain cells that die off in Parkinson's disease, and they successfully grafted these into monkeys' brains to reverse movement problems caused by Parkinson's. The breakthrough raises the prospect that, one day, freshly grown dopamine-producing cells could be transplanted into human patients to treat Parkinson's disease.

Stem cell research is controversial, however. This is because to get stem cells, scientists have to use an embryo (the early phase of a baby growing inside its mother). This embryo either has already been conceived, or otherwise scientists make a copy of an embryo created from a cell from the patient's body and a donated egg. In both cases, scientists have to destroy an embryo to get stem cells from it. Some people say that destroying an embryo is like taking a human life.

Physical therapy
This Parkinson's patient is working with a physical therapist. Though it is not a cure, many people who have Parkinson's disease are able to improve their quality of life through physical therapy.

Arthritis

The word arthritis is from the Greek words for "joint" (arthro) and "inflammation" (-itis), and it describes a condition that makes joints sore and swollen. Bones are connected to other bones at the joints, and joints are the body parts that allow bones to move.

Osteoarthritis facts

The following are some interesting facts about osteoarthritis:

- Osteoarthritis is one of the 10 most disabling diseases in developed countries.
- Worldwide estimates are that 9.6 percent of men and 18 percent of women over 60 years old have osteoarthritis. About 45 percent of women over 65 have symptoms, and more than 80 percent of people who reach the age of 70 have it.
- Four out of every five people with osteoarthritis have limitations in movement, and 25 percent cannot perform important daily activities.

Osteoarthritis is the most common form of arthritis. It usually occurs in old age, although it can develop at any age as a result of an injury or another joint-related condition. As people get older, the cartilage that once covered the ends of bones and made them smooth slowly wears away, leaving the bones rubbing together. This wear and tear is thought to interact with genetic factors to contribute to osteoarthritis. Osteoarthritis makes the joints very stiff and painful and can make moving around difficult. The body cannot heal itself, because the ability of tissues to repair themselves also decreases with age. However, today, many joints can be replaced by artificial ones.

AMAZING BUT TRUE!

Arthritis in children

Arthritis is usually associated with older people, but one form—juvenile arthritis—affects children. Juvenile arthritis is defined as any form of arthritis found in a person under the age of 18. This condition affects about 1 in 1,000 children, and is considered one of the most common childhood diseases in the United States.

Risk factors and treatment

Although scientists are not entirely sure what causes osteoarthritis, apart from wear and tear over a lifetime, there are risk factors that people can address to reduce their chances of getting it. Osteoarthritis is more common in people who are overweight than in people who maintain a healthy weight as they get older. Being physically active also helps, as it keeps joints strong and flexible—although people should also recognize that if they feel achy and stiff, they should rest rather than put more strain on their joints.

For people who have osteoarthritis, there are treatment options. They can take medicine to reduce the pain, have periods of rest, lose weight, and exercise. Some people also have injections of corticosteroids, which are artificial hormones that reduce inflammation. In the most severe cases, people have surgery to replace important joints such as the hip or knee.

Busy joints

Since it is associated with aging, osteoarthritis usually affects joints that people use the most over a lifetime, such as the knees, hips, fingers, and lower spine.

Rheumatoid arthritis

Rheumatoid arthritis is a more severe, but less common, form of arthritis than osteoarthritis. It occurs when the body's immune system attacks and destroys the tissues surrounding the affected joints. This causes pain and swelling and can lead to a reduction in movement and the breakdown of bone and cartilage. It tends to strike during adulthood, between the ages of 20 and 40, and is a chronic condition that leads to long-term joint damage, chronic pain, loss of function, and disability.

Hip replacement

The hip joint consists of a ball at the top of the thighbone that fits into a rounded socket in the pelvis. When a hip is damaged—for example, by arthritis or a fracture—even simple things like walking or getting in and out of a chair can become painful and difficult. Some sufferers are still in pain when they are lying in bed! One year after a hip fracture, 60 percent of patients are limited in activities such as eating, dressing, and using the bathroom; 80 percent are no longer able to perform activities such as shopping, gardening, and climbing stairs.

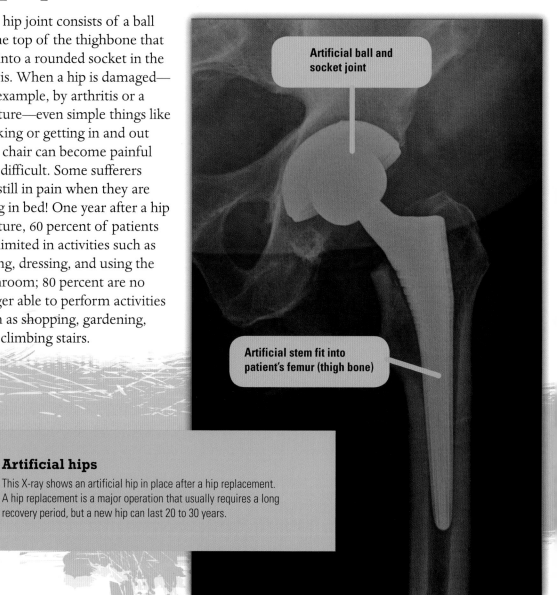

Artificial ball and socket joint

Artificial stem fit into patient's femur (thigh bone)

Artificial hips

This X-ray shows an artificial hip in place after a hip replacement. A hip replacement is a major operation that usually requires a long recovery period, but a new hip can last 20 to 30 years.

About half of all cases of hip fractures are fixed with plates and screws or rods, and the rest require surgery to replace the joint with an artificial hip. In a total hip replacement operation, the surgeon replaces the worn head of the thighbone with a metal or ceramic ball mounted on a stem. The socket is resurfaced with a polyethylene (plastic) or polyethylene-lined metal cup.

In the past, a damaged hip would have severely restricted a person's life. Today, modern surgical techniques like hip replacement enable people to deal with health problems and go on leading active lives for far longer than people could have imagined 50 years ago.

Case study: Double hip replacement

Norman Lane, 63, had a double hip replacement due to problems from osteoarthritis. He said:

I used to be a soccer player and ran around 80 miles a week until I started to have problems with my hips when I was around 40. The doctor diagnosed osteoarthritis. At first it wasn't too bad, but gradually things got so painful that I couldn't turn over in bed at night, let alone run. The surgeon said both my hips were "shot" and suggested a double hip replacement, which I had done in 1998.

The operation lasted eight hours. The day after, it took me 20 minutes to walk to the end of the bed and back. It seemed impossible that I would ever run again, but I was determined. I didn't want to die with my new hips unused! I was in the hospital for a week. It was painful at first but I stopped taking painkillers after two days and the pain gradually went away over the course of about a month.

After a month, I was riding a bike. After six months, I started to do some gentle running and very gradually built it up over the course of a year. After 18 months, I ran the Majorca marathon in 3 hours and 14 minutes, winning the international over-50 category. I did the New York and London marathons the next year.

AMAZING BUT TRUE!

Heavyweight hips

The hip is one of the body's largest weight-bearing joints, and being overweight has a negative impact on the joints of the lower body. For every extra pound of body weight a person carries, the hip and knee joints have five times the impact. That means that five extra pounds adds 25 pounds of impact every time a person takes a step!

Health Development

It is inevitable that, as people get older, their bodies age and become more prone to health problems. A young adult's body is made up of around 100 trillion cells. Some of them, such as brain cells, are hardly ever replaced when they wear out; others are constantly replaced by existing cells that divide and multiply to make new ones.

The problem is that even cells that have the ability to replace themselves can only do this a certain number of times before they die, too. That is why the body's ability to repair damaged tissue decreases with age, and why older people take much longer to recover from accidents and disease than young people. As more cells are lost or damaged, people start to show outward signs of aging, such as thinner skin. It also becomes harder for the body to repair itself and stay healthy—and this limits everyone's lifespan.

AMAZING BUT TRUE!

Super cell production

The body is repairing itself and parts keep growing throughout a lifetime. By the time you finish reading this sentence, 50 million of your cells will have died and been replaced!

Increasing lifespan

Improvements in medicine, diet, and awareness of how to keep ourselves healthy have increased the average lifespan, and they continue to do so as poorer countries develop and standards of living there increase. As the world's population continues to grow and the number of older people in the world increases, the number of people suffering from illness and disease will also inevitably increase. The increasing number of older and sicker people will increase the costs of health care extensively, and this will become a major issue in the future.

Healthy for life

In spite of the fact that aging inevitably weakens and changes the human body, there are many different health outcomes for individuals. Some people suffer from a debilitating disease from youth or early adulthood; others remain healthy and active into their nineties.

The health we enjoy throughout our lives is due to several factors—a combination of genetics, environment, and luck. In the future, genetic screening may be able to tell us what conditions we are most likely to develop, so that we can change our lifestyles and environments and take action to avoid those outcomes. Until then, the best option is to make positive choices to maintain and improve health—for example, by getting regular exercise, eating a healthy diet, and avoiding risky behaviors such as smoking. That should give your changing body the resources and chances it needs to stay healthy.

Take care of yourself!
By taking care of their bodies, people have a better chance of staying healthy and living life to the fullest.

Quiz

Find out how much you remember about health and disease by completing this quiz. You can find the answers on page 63.

1. Genes spell out, in a chemical code called BNA, all the instructions needed to make us who we are.
   True or false?

2. What is the name of the system mainly controlled by white blood cells, which tag and destroy bacteria or viruses when they get inside our blood?

3. When is a baby's immune system weakest?
   a.) at birth   b.) at 6 months   c.) at 12 months

4. What is the name for the process by which a small amount of a killed or weakened pathogen is injected into the body to create immunity?

   a.) vaccination   b.) antibody   c.) bacteria

5. What is the main difference between viruses and bacteria?

6. What percentage of common infections are spread by dirty or infected hands?
   a.) 50 percent   b.) 100 percent   c.) 80 percent

7. An allergy is an overreaction of the immune system to a substance that is harmful to most people.
True or false?

8. A newborn's skeleton is made of a flexible material called …
a.) mucus   b.) bone   c.) cartilage

9. Why is it important for young people to have a diet that is rich in calcium?

10. What is the hardest substance in the body?
a.) bone   b.) fingernails   c.) tooth enamel

11. Which part of the body is directly affected by alcohol?
a.) brain and central nervous system
b.) respiratory system
c.) circulatory system

12. What is the best way to avoid STDs (sexually transmitted diseases)?

13. Which disease is the world's major cause of death?
a.) cancer   b.) heart disease   c.) flu

14. What simple action should people take to reduce their risk of the bone disease osteoporosis?

15. Cataracts that affect sight in old age occur in which part of the eye?
a.) retina   b.) lens   c.) optic nerve

Timeline

1628
William Harvey describes how blood is pumped throughout the body by the heart.

1676
Anton van Leeuwenhoek refines the microscope and discovers blood cells.

1796
Edward Jenner develops the smallpox vaccine.

1818
British obstetrician James Blundell performs the first successful transfusion of human blood.

1867
Joseph Lister advocates the use of antiseptics to prevent infections after surgery.

1952
Paul Zoll develops the first cardiac pacemaker to control an irregular heartbeat.

1951
A study links smoking and lung cancer for the first time.

1948
The World Health Organization is founded by the United Nations.

1945
The first vaccine for influenza is created.

1928
Alexander Fleming discovers penicillin.

1953
James Watson and Francis Crick describe the structure of DNA.

1957
The Asian flu sweeps the world, causing an estimated two million deaths.

1964
The first vaccine for measles is created.

1967
The first vaccine for mumps is created.

1967
Dr. Christiaan Barnard performs the first human heart transplant.

2007
Scientists discover how to use human skin cells to create embryonic stem cells.

2002
The first outbreaks of severe acute respiratory syndrome (SARS) occur in Asia and Canada.

2001
The Measles Initiative is launched; by October 2007, overall global measles deaths will fall by 68 percent.

1992
The first vaccine for hepatitis A is created.

1870s Louis Pasteur and Robert Koch establish the theory that specific diseases are caused by specific germs.	**1879** The first vaccine for the disease cholera is created.	**1897** The first vaccine for the plague is created.	**1906** Frederick Hopkins describes vitamins and the fact that they are essential to health.	**1913** Dr. Paul Dudley White pioneers the use of the electrocardiograph to diagnose heart conditions.

1926 The first vaccine for whooping cough is created.	**1924** The first active vaccine for tetanus is created.	**1922** Insulin is first used to treat diabetes.	**1921** The first vaccine for tuberculosis (TB) is created.	**1918–1919** An influenza pandemic leads to the death of 50 million people.

1970 The first vaccine for rubella is created.	**1974** The first vaccine for chicken pox is created.	**1977** The first vaccine for pneumonia is created.	**1978** The first test-tube baby is born.	**1978** The first vaccine for meningitis is created.

1989 A hepatitis C infection is identified for the first time.	**1985** Willem J. Kolff invents the artificial kidney dialysis machine.	**1983** HIV, the virus that causes AIDS, is identified.	**1981** The first vaccine for hepatitis B is created.	**1980** The World Health Organization announces that smallpox is eradicated.

Glossary

adolescence period following the start of puberty when a young person develops from a child into an adult

AIDS short for "acquired immune deficiency syndrome," it is a condition that makes the immune system too weak to fight infections

allergen substance causing an allergic reaction

allergy when a person's immune system reacts to substances that are normally harmless

antibiotic medicine such as penicillin that prevents the growth of or kills microorganisms

antibody substance produced by the immune system to attack bacteria or virus cells

artery blood vessel carrying blood containing large amounts of oxygen from the heart to other parts of the body

arthritis disease that makes joints of the body (like the knees) swollen and painful

autoimmune disorder condition in which the immune system reacts against substances and tissues that are normally present in the body

bacterium (plural: **bacteria**) type of single-celled organism found everywhere, some of which can cause disease

cancer disease in which some of the body's cells divide in an uncontrolled manner

cartilage strong white tissue—for example, the tissue in joints that stops bones from rubbing together

cell basic unit of life. Organisms are formed from a single, several, or many cells.

cholesterol fatty substance found in body tissues

contagious disease that spreads easily from one person to another

developed country country with high levels of development such as modern hospitals and transportation networks and in which people usually have a high income by world standards

developing country country with lower levels of development such as poor roads and insufficient schools in which people usually have a low income by world standards

diabetes disease where someone has high levels of sugar in their blood

diarrhea condition in which the sufferer has frequent and watery bowel movements

DNA short for "deoxyribonucleic acid," this material carries genetic information

fertility state of being fertile, or capable of having babies

fever medical condition in which a person has a higher than normal temperature

fracture break in a bone

gene something that parents pass to offspring during reproduction and that passes on characteristics

gene therapy experimental technique that uses genes to treat or prevent disease. In the future, this technique may allow doctors to treat a disorder by inserting a gene into a patient's cells instead of using drugs or surgery.

gland organ in the body that releases particular chemical substances for use by the body

heredity physical or mental characteristics that are passed from parent to child

HIV short for "human immunodeficiency virus." This is the virus that causes AIDS.

hormonal relating to hormones

hormone chemical produced by one part of the body to send messages that affect cells in other parts

immune system system consisting of special cells, tissues, and organs that defends the body against disease

infertility when a couple cannot conceive (get pregnant) despite having regular unprotected sex

joint point at which two or more bones meet

malnourished not being provided with adequate nourishment

menstrual cycle monthly cycle in which older girls and women have periods. Every month, the uterus lines itself in preparation for pregnancy, and when pregnancy does not happen, the lining is shed.

microorganism microscopic organism, such as a bacterium or virus

mucus slimy substance found in the nose and throat—for example, when a person has a cold

mutation permanent change in the DNA sequence of a gene

nutrient substance in food that helps people live and grow

organ part of the body that has a particular job to do, such as the heart or brain

pathogen something that causes disease or illness in the body

puberty time in a person's life when their body gradually changes from a child's into an adult's

respiration process by which energy is released from glucose in food using oxygen for the body's cells to use, in order to keep the body working

saliva fluid (sometimes called spit) produced by glands in the mouth that moisten food making it easier to swallow. It also aids in digesting some types of food.

tissue cells grouped together in the body, forming parts of the body such as muscles and nerves

vaccination use of vaccines to prevent specific diseases

vaccine substance used to encourage the body to make antibodies that provide immunity against one or several diseases

virus microorganism that can cause disease

X-ray type of radiation used to make pictures of the bones inside the body—for example, to check for fractures

Find Out More

Books

Claybourne, Anna. *Life Processes* (*The Web of Life*). Chicago: Raintree, 2012.

DiConsiglio, John. *Superbugs* (*Hot Topics*). Chicago: Heinemann Library, 2012.

Hardyman, Robyn. *Exercise* (*Being Healthy, Feeling Great*). New York: PowerKids, 2010.

Levete, Sarah. *Health and Disease* (*Headline Issues*). Chicago: Heinemann Library, 2009.

Townsend, John. *101 Things You Didn't Know About Your Body* (*101*).
     Chicago: Raintree, 2012.

Web sites

www.amnh.org/ology/index.php?channel=genetics
This web site created by the American Museum of Natural History has quizzes, facts, and projects relating to genetics.

www.healthyteeth.org
This web site provides lots of information about issues related to healthy teeth, from braces to bad breath.

kidshealth.org/kid/stay_healthy/index.html
KidsHealth offers a clear, fun guide to staying healthy, with illustrations and animations. You can also search the KidsHealth web site for information about specific diseases.

pbskids.org/itsmylife/body/index.html
This PBS site has information on a range of subjects, including food, puberty, smoking, and drug abuse.

Places to visit

The Exploratorium
3601 Lyon Street
San Francisco, California 94123
www.exploratorium.edu
The "Traits of Life" interactive exhibit explores the common features of all living things, and there are also sections on sight and hearing.

The Health Museum
1515 Hermann Drive
Houston, Texas 77004
www.mhms.org
This museum offers interactive exhibits about the body, cells, and health in which you can take a walking tour through a human body, including a walk-in eyeball and cell!

Topics to research

Pandemics

A pandemic is a disease that spreads around the world. In the past, pandemics like the plague and flu killed millions of people. Vaccinations and improved health care and sanitation seem to have made such massive events a thing of the past. However, new strains of viruses have caused major scares and spread quickly, because world travel is so easy today. Find out about the swine flu pandemic that began in Mexico in 2009 and spread quickly from country to country before it died down in 2010.

All about aspirin

Why is aspirin known as the "wonder drug"? What are the 80 million aspirin tablets taken every year across the world used to treat? What side effects can this drug have? The first aspirin was made from willow bark. Find out what aspirin is made from today and about other medicines that are, or were, derived from plants.

Health and choices

Why do so many people of all ages do things that they know are bad for their health? Why do people start smoking when they know it could kill them? For example, why do some people lie in the sun day after day without protection, when they know such behavior could cause skin cancer? It is a problem that challenges doctors and governments all over the world. What do you think? How can people be persuaded to take better care of their bodies?

Quiz answers (see pages 56–57)

1) False: It is "DNA," not "BNA."

2) The immune system.

3) b.

4) a.

5) Viruses cannot multiply on their own.

6) c.

7) False: It is a reaction to a substance that is harmless to most people.

8) c.

9) To build strong bones.

10) c.

11) a.

12) Never have unprotected sex (sex without a condom).

13) b.

14) Get regular exercise.

15) b.

Index